THE AWAKENING
Dream Notebook

www.oneneighbor.net

COPYRIGHT NOTICE:

The Awakening Dream Notebook
Copyright © 2020 by Lem Wallace

Cover photo @lightstock.com

Scripture taken from the NEW AMERICAN STANDARD BIBLE®,
Copyright © 1960,1962,1963,1968,1971,1972,1973,1975,1977,1995
by The Lockman Foundation. Used by permission.

THIS DOCUMENT IS PROTECTED UNDER UNITED STATES INTERNATIONAL COPYRIGHT LAWS.

THIS DOCUMENT MAY NOT BE SHARED, MANIPULATED, COPIED, REPRODUCED, USED OR ALTERED IN ANY FORM OR BY ANY MEANS, INCLUDING MECHANICAL, ELECTRICAL, PHOTOCOPYING, OR OTHERWISE WITHOUT THE PERMISSION OF THE AUTHOR.

UNAUTHORIZED USE OF THIS DOCUMENT IS VIOLATION OF COPYRIGHT AND PUNISHABLE BY LAW.

www.oneneighbor.net
ONE NEIGHBOR PUBLISHING

Introduction

Did you know we were all born with the ability to dream? As God carefully formed us in our mother's womb (Psalm 139:13), it shouldn't be surprising that we spent most of our time in utero dreaming and in the Father's presence. Dreaming is our first language of communication with God. Even after birth, dreaming is an important part of our lives. Those who have watched a newborn slip into a milk-induced sleep have witnessed the rapid eye movement known as R.E.M. The typical sleep cycles are not needed for them to begin dreaming.[1]

Consider the idea of dreaming being a form of communication with God. Many of us can admit that with busy schedules and demands of life, that we carve little or no time with God. Dreaming may be the only time when we are isolated from all distractions and able to experience quality time with God.

What good are dreams?
Dreams can be very useful. When you dream God can impart wisdom, help you solve nerve-racking problems, and guide you how to intercede for others. Your dreams are not only good for your spiritual development, but has physical benefits as well. According to medical researchers, if you learn a task and then sleep you may be ten times better at that activity than if you had stayed awake. Dreaming helps your brain make sense of new information. When you are resting, it gives your body time to heal and repair itself, while your mind is being restored and refreshed. Sometimes dreams can be concise with clarity while most times they express themselves in the subtle language of symbols, metaphors, and a variety of images attached to scenes.

What are sources of our dreams?
Dreams can come from three main sources: God, Satan, and the soul.

Dreams from God are not always filled with light, but can be dark (Daniel 4:5). Dark dreams will often reveal and warn us of plans of the enemy. How can you tell if a dream is from God? Look at the result of the dream. God sends dreams to grow us in a certain area, strengthen our spirit, give understanding, and grow our relationship with Him.

Similarly, dreams from the enemy are not always dark, but can fool us with brightness. The Bible says that Satan sometimes masquerades as an angel of light (2 Corinthians 11:14). Satan will use nightmares to create fear to hinder our dreaming. He wants to interfere with our line of communication with God. Remember God's intentions are not to harm you (Jeremiah 29:11).

©2020 One Neighbor Publishing LLC

The third source of dreams is neither God or Satan, but from our soul. A soul dream is heavily influenced by our own fears, desires, and emotions. It is very important, with any dream, that we analyze it (1 Thessalonians 5:21) to see if it is from God or our own mind (Jeremiah 23:16).

Who does God give dreams to?
Both believers and unbelievers can receive dreams from God.

UNBELIEVERS

Dreamer	Scripture	Dreamer	Scripture
Abimelech	Genesis 20	Unnamed man	Judges 7:13
Pharaoh's cup bearer	Genesis 40	Nebuchadnezzar	Daniel 2; Daniel 4
Pharaoh's baker	Genesis 40	Magi	Matthew 2:12
Pharaoh	Genesis 41	Pontius Pilate's wife	Matthew 27:19

BELIEVERS

Dreamer	Scripture	Dreamer	Scripture
Jacob	Genesis 23:12; Genesis 31:10-11	Solomon	1 Kings 3:5-15
Laban	Genesis 31:24	Daniel	Daniel 7
Joseph	Genesis 37:1-10	Joseph	Matthew 1:18-24; Matthew 2:13, 22

Are dreams the same as visions?
Dreams and visions are very similar. The biggest difference is dreams are filled with symbolism while visions are more literal. Also, dreams only occur when you are unconscious. Visions can happen when you are either awake or asleep.

Why should you record your dreams?
Dreams, no matter how fresh in our minds when we awaken, can quickly fade as the day progresses. Get into the habit of recording them immediately. It is a great way to document God's faithfulness. You will also be able to look back and

see warnings and dangers averted.

God will also reward your diligence. The more you commit to recording your dreams, the more dreams He will give you. God will honor your efforts to seek Him and understanding (Deuteronomy 4:29; Proverbs 8:17). Remember God wants to spend time with you and only He can reveal the true meaning of His messages to you.

How to use this dream notebook
Before start recording your dream, it's important for you to remember to write in the date and title your dream. The title may help you remember the events in your dream. For each section, answer the questions and fill in the charts.

Dream interpretations are not a one-size fits all. Because each person is unique and we all have our own experiences, likes, and dislikes, there is no specific formula used to interpret. The meaning of colors, people, locations, and symbols will be unique to each dreamer. We each have our own dream language. However, because dreaming is how we communicate with God, it is important that we learn His language. This will take time, consistency, and time in prayer.

A few things to consider...
1. Title your dream according to what's happening in the dream. This will help with recalling details.

2. Where are you in the dream? If you are an observer, more than likely the dream is about someone or something else. If you are a participant in the dream, but not the main focus, then the dream is about something you are involved in. If you are the main focus and activity revolves around you, the dream is about something happening or will happen in your life.

3. If you have difficulty deciding what or who the main focus is, picture removing that thing or person from the dream. Does the dream still make sense?

4. Is the dream recurring? If the dream is one you have had before, there is something important in it that needs your attention.

5. Your emotion or feeling while in the dream will help you determine how to interpret the symbols, whether you look at the positive or negative meanings.

6. Colors are important in your dreams. Don't overlook them. They either mean something or help with interpretation.

©2020 One Neighbor Publishing LLC

How long will it take to interpret your dream?
Dream interpretation can take minutes, hours, or days, and should never be rushed. You may also find that certain aspects of a dream may remain "locked" until God reveals a little more to you months or even years down the road.

Get creative
Recording your dream with pen and paper is not the only way. There are other ways to record your dreams, such as, sketching with colored pens and pencils, painting, using clay, and any other creative outlet you enjoy. If writing is your preferred way of recording, consider grouping elements, diagramming (similar to sentence diagramming), mapping, writing in patterns, or emphasizing key words. In trying different ways to illustrate your dream, you may find the more you remember and recall new details.

This guide is in no way an exhaustive resource. It is my hope that this dream notebook will encourage you to pay more attention to your dreams and grow your relationship with God. Ask God to release dreams to you and the ability to remember them. God loves you and desires to spend time with you. This is only the beginning.

DREAM.
RECORD.
PRAY.
INTERPRET.
REPEAT.

End Notes

1. Lifenews.com. (2013, July 2). Unborn Babies Can Dream in the Womb, Will Abortion be Their Nightmare? Retrieved from https://www.lifenews.com/2013/07/02/unborn-babies-feel-pain-and-can-dream-in-the-womb-lets-protect-them/

DATE: 8/12/2020 **TITLE:** Peter's Dream

Describe your dream in 3-5 sentences.

A dark green plant wearing a dirty crown is squeezing the earth. Its vines are wrapped tightly. A lion with the body of a lamb attacked the plant.

Scene(s): Where is your dream taking place?

Location	Means to You	Positive	Negative
space	above Earth		

What role do YOU play in dream? [X] Observer   [ ] Participant

List the important people and things in your dream.

Person/Thing	Representative	Positive	Negative
Peter	Church		
Earth	world		those that do not know Christ
plant	virus/SYNVID		
lion/lamb	Christ		

©2020 One Neighbor Publishing LLC

Color(s): What colors were in your dream?

Color	Means to You	Positive	Negative
dark green	vegetables	growth, prosperity	(jealousy, pride)
white	clean	(holiness)	religious spirit
purple	favorite drink	authority, royalty	(false authority)

What was on your mind or heart prior to falling asleep? Were you reading or watching anything that found its way in your dream?
N/A. Peter was in a coma for 8 days. He has no memory of the boating accident.

List any current issues or decisions pending closure or guidance.
N/A.

Is this a recurring dream? Yes ☐ No ☒

If yes, what details stood out?

What emotion(s) were you feeling in the dream?
Confused when couldn't move arms and legs. Scared at the sight of the plant. Peace when the lion with lamb's body appeared.

©2020 One Neighbor Publishing LLC

Write/Sketch/Illustrate Dream

Peter was floating. He couldn't feel his arms and legs. The earth appeared slowly in front of him - fuzzy at first. Glimpses of the water and land could be seen as clouds passed over.

Peter's view sharpened. He immediately saw a large dark green plant. It wore a tarnished crown on its head. The head pulsed like a heartbeat. With each pulse, the plant's vines wrapped around the earth squeezed tighter.

Peter gasped. The plant turned its head towards him. It had no eyes, but a large mouth. When the plant opened its mouth purple smoke came out. One of the plant's vines came at Peter. Out of no where a white lion with a lamb's body jumped from above. It tore the plant to pieces.

Pray and ask God....write your interpretation below.
- What is the meaning of the dream?
- What is the purpose of the dream?
- How do I apply the dream to my life?

Peter = Church
Plant = SYNVID
lion/lamb = Christ
Earth = world

The Church has been paralyzed by confusion during this season. The world was to be the Church's mission field, but lost sight of it. As the Church refocuses its vision, a new enemy has taken hold - SYNVID. SYNVID was created by jealous and prideful men with their own agenda. SYNVID squeezes the earth/people of the world under false authority.

The Church should not fear the virus. It is man made and those behind it cannot see the things of God. Because those behind the virus have their finger on the pulse of the world, they have the world in a death grip using deception (by word of mouth/media) and fear. They may strike at the Church, but we will not be overcome. Jesus Christ, in His authority and Truth, will reveal the lies and bring peace.

Purpose/Application - Message to the Church...

What other questions do you still have about your dream?

DATE: **TITLE:**

Describe your dream in 3-5 sentences.

Scene(s): Where is your dream taking place?

Location	Means to You	Positive	Negative

What role do YOU play in dream? ☐ Observer ☐ Participant

List the important people and things in your dream.

Person/Thing	Representative	Positive	Negative

©2020 One Neighbor Publishing LLC

Color(s): What colors were in your dream?

Color	Means to You	Positive	Negative

What was on your mind or heart prior to falling asleep? Were you reading or watching anything that found its way in your dream?

List any current issues or decisions pending closure or guidance.

Is this a recurring dream?   Yes ☐   No ☐

If yes, what details stood out?

What emotion(s) were you feeling in the dream?

©2020 One Neighbor Publishing LLC

Write/Sketch/Illustrate Dream

©2020 One Neighbor Publishing LLC

Pray and ask God....write your interpretation below.
- What is the meaning of the dream?
- What is the purpose of the dream?
- How do I apply the dream to my life?

What other questions do you still have about your dream?

©2020 One Neighbor Publishing LLC

DATE: **TITLE:**

Describe your dream in 3-5 sentences.

Scene(s): Where is your dream taking place?

Location	Means to You	Positive	Negative

What role do YOU play in dream? ☐ Observer ☐ Participant

List the important people and things in your dream.

Person/Thing	Representative	Positive	Negative

©2020 One Neighbor Publishing LLC

Color(s): What colors were in your dream?

Color	Means to You	Positive	Negative

What was on your mind or heart prior to falling asleep? Were you reading or watching anything that found its way in your dream?

List any current issues or decisions pending closure or guidance.

Is this a recurring dream? Yes ☐   No ☐

If yes, what details stood out?

What emotion(s) were you feeling in the dream?

©2020 One Neighbor Publishing LLC

Write/Sketch/Illustrate Dream

©2020 One Neighbor Publishing LLC

Pray and ask God....write your interpretation below.
- What is the meaning of the dream?
- What is the purpose of the dream?
- How do I apply the dream to my life?

What other questions do you still have about your dream?

©2020 One Neighbor Publishing LLC

DATE: TITLE:

Describe your dream in 3-5 sentences.

Scene(s): Where is your dream taking place?

Location	Means to You	Positive	Negative

What role do YOU play in dream?   ☐ Observer   ☐ Participant

List the important people and things in your dream.

Person/Thing	Representative	Positive	Negative

©2020 One Neighbor Publishing LLC

Color(s): What colors were in your dream?

Color	Means to You	Positive	Negative

What was on your mind or heart prior to falling asleep? Were you reading or watching anything that found its way in your dream?

List any current issues or decisions pending closure or guidance.

Is this a recurring dream?   Yes ☐   No ☐

If yes, what details stood out?

What emotion(s) were you feeling in the dream?

©2020 One Neighbor Publishing LLC

Write/Sketch/Illustrate Dream

©2020 One Neighbor Publishing LLC

Pray and ask God....write your interpretation below.
- What is the meaning of the dream?
- What is the purpose of the dream?
- How do I apply the dream to my life?

What other questions do you still have about your dream?

DATE: TITLE:

Describe your dream in 3-5 sentences.

Scene(s): Where is your dream taking place?

Location	Means to You	Positive	Negative

What role do YOU <u>play</u> in dream? ☐ Observer ☐ Participant

List the important people and things in your dream.

Person/Thing	Representative	Positive	Negative

©2020 One Neighbor Publishing LLC

Color(s): What colors were in your dream?

Color	Means to You	Positive	Negative

What was on your mind or heart prior to falling asleep? Were you reading or watching anything that found its way in your dream?

List any current issues or decisions pending closure or guidance.

Is this a recurring dream? Yes ☐ No ☐

If yes, what details stood out?

What emotion(s) were you feeling in the dream?

©2020 One Neighbor Publishing LLC

Write/Sketch/Illustrate Dream

©2020 One Neighbor Publishing LLC

Pray and ask God....write your interpretation below.
- What is the meaning of the dream?
- What is the purpose of the dream?
- How do I apply the dream to my life?

What other questions do you still have about your dream?

DATE: TITLE:

Describe your dream in 3-5 sentences.

Scene(s): Where is your dream taking place?

Location	Means to You	Positive	Negative

What role do YOU <u>play</u> in dream?   ☐ Observer   ☐ Participant

List the important people and things in your dream.

Person/Thing	Representative	Positive	Negative

©2020 One Neighbor Publishing LLC

Color(s): What colors were in your dream?

Color	Means to You	Positive	Negative

What was on your mind or heart prior to falling asleep? Were you reading or watching anything that found its way in your dream?

List any current issues or decisions pending closure or guidance.

Is this a recurring dream?   Yes ☐   No ☐

If yes, what details stood out?

What emotion(s) were you feeling in the dream?

©2020 One Neighbor Publishing LLC

Write/Sketch/Illustrate Dream

©2020 One Neighbor Publishing LLC

Pray and ask God....write your interpretation below.
- What is the meaning of the dream?
- What is the purpose of the dream?
- How do I apply the dream to my life?

What other questions do you still have about your dream?

DATE: **TITLE:**

Describe your dream in 3-5 sentences.

Scene(s): Where is your dream taking place?

Location	Means to You	Positive	Negative

What role do YOU <u>play</u> in dream? ☐ Observer ☐ Participant

List the important people and things in your dream.

Person/Thing	Representative	Positive	Negative

©2020 One Neighbor Publishing LLC

Color(s): What colors were in your dream?

Color	Means to You	Positive	Negative

What was on your mind or heart prior to falling asleep? Were you reading or watching anything that found its way in your dream?

List any current issues or decisions pending closure or guidance.

Is this a recurring dream? Yes ☐ No ☐

If yes, what details stood out?

What emotion(s) were you feeling in the dream?

©2020 One Neighbor Publishing LLC

Write/Sketch/Illustrate Dream

©2020 One Neighbor Publishing LLC

Pray and ask God....write your interpretation below.
- What is the meaning of the dream?
- How do I apply the dream to my life?
- What is the purpose of the dream?

What other questions do you still have about your dream?

Color(s): What colors were in your dream?

Color	Means to You	Positive	Negative

What was on your mind or heart prior to falling asleep? Were you reading or watching anything that found its way in your dream?

List any current issues or decisions pending closure or guidance.

Is this a recurring dream?   Yes ☐   No ☐

If yes, what details stood out?

What emotion(s) were you feeling in the dream?

©2020 One Neighbor Publishing LLC

Write/Sketch/Illustrate Dream

©2020 One Neighbor Publishing LLC

Pray and ask God....write your interpretation below.
- What is the meaning of the dream?
- What is the purpose of the dream?
- How do I apply the dream to my life?

What other questions do you still have about your dream?

DATE: **TITLE:**

Describe your dream in 3-5 sentences.

Scene(s): Where is your dream taking place?

Location	Means to You	Positive	Negative

What role do YOU <u>play</u> in dream? ☐ Observer   ☐ Participant

List the important people and things in your dream.

Person/Thing	Representative	Positive	Negative

©2020 One Neighbor Publishing LLC

Color(s): What colors were in your dream?

Color	Means to You	Positive	Negative

What was on your mind or heart prior to falling asleep? Were you reading or watching anything that found its way in your dream?

List any current issues or decisions pending closure or guidance.

Is this a recurring dream? Yes ☐   No ☐

If yes, what details stood out?

What emotion(s) were you feeling in the dream?

©2020 One Neighbor Publishing LLC

Write/Sketch/Illustrate Dream

©2020 One Neighbor Publishing LLC

Pray and ask God....write your interpretation below.
- What is the meaning of the dream?
- What is the purpose of the dream?
- How do I apply the dream to my life?

What other questions do you still have about your dream?

DATE: TITLE:

Describe your dream in 3-5 sentences.

Scene(s): Where is your dream taking place?

Location	Means to You	Positive	Negative

What role do YOU <u>play</u> in dream?   ☐ Observer   ☐ Participant

List the important people and things in your dream.

Person/Thing	Representative	Positive	Negative

©2020 One Neighbor Publishing LLC

Color(s): What colors were in your dream?

Color	Means to You	Positive	Negative

What was on your mind or heart prior to falling asleep? Were you reading or watching anything that found its way in your dream?

List any current issues or decisions pending closure or guidance.

Is this a recurring dream?   Yes ☐   No ☐

If yes, what details stood out?

What emotion(s) were you feeling in the dream?

©2020 One Neighbor Publishing LLC

Write/Sketch/Illustrate Dream

Pray and ask God....write your interpretation below.
- What is the meaning of the dream?
- What is the purpose of the dream?
- How do I apply the dream to my life?

What other questions do you still have about your dream?

DATE:　　　　　　　　　　TITLE:

Describe your dream in 3-5 sentences.

Scene(s): Where is your dream taking place?

Location	Means to You	Positive	Negative

What role do YOU <u>play</u> in dream?　☐ Observer　☐ Participant

List the important people and things in your dream.

Person/Thing	Representative	Positive	Negative

©2020 One Neighbor Publishing LLC

Color(s): What colors were in your dream?

Color	Means to You	Positive	Negative

What was on your mind or heart prior to falling asleep? Were you reading or watching anything that found its way in your dream?

List any current issues or decisions pending closure or guidance.

Is this a recurring dream?   Yes ☐   No ☐

If yes, what details stood out?

What emotion(s) were you feeling in the dream?

©2020 One Neighbor Publishing LLC

Write/Sketch/Illustrate Dream

©2020 One Neighbor Publishing LLC

Pray and ask God....write your interpretation below.
- What is the meaning of the dream?
- What is the purpose of the dream?
- How do I apply the dream to my life?

What other questions do you still have about your dream?

©2020 One Neighbor Publishing LLC

DATE: **TITLE:**

Describe your dream in 3-5 sentences.

Scene(s): Where is your dream taking place?

Location	Means to You	Positive	Negative

What role do YOU play in dream? ☐ Observer ☐ Participant

List the important people and things in your dream.

Person/Thing	Representative	Positive	Negative

©2020 One Neighbor Publishing LLC

Color(s): What colors were in your dream?

Color	Means to You	Positive	Negative

What was on your mind or heart prior to falling asleep? Were you reading or watching anything that found its way in your dream?

List any current issues or decisions pending closure or guidance.

Is this a recurring dream?   Yes ☐   No ☐

If yes, what details stood out?

What emotion(s) were you feeling in the dream?

©2020 One Neighbor Publishing LLC

Write/Sketch/Illustrate Dream

©2020 One Neighbor Publishing LLC

Pray and ask God....write your interpretation below.
- What is the meaning of the dream?
- What is the purpose of the dream?
- How do I apply the dream to my life?

What other questions do you still have about your dream?

DATE: TITLE:

Describe your dream in 3-5 sentences.

Scene(s): Where is your dream taking place?

Location	Means to You	Positive	Negative

What role do YOU play in dream?   ☐ Observer   ☐ Participant

List the important people and things in your dream.

Person/Thing	Representative	Positive	Negative

©2020 One Neighbor Publishing LLC

Color(s): What colors were in your dream?

Color	Means to You	Positive	Negative

What was on your mind or heart prior to falling asleep? Were you reading or watching anything that found its way in your dream?

List any current issues or decisions pending closure or guidance.

Is this a recurring dream?   Yes ☐   No ☐

If yes, what details stood out?

What emotion(s) were you feeling in the dream?

©2020 One Neighbor Publishing LLC

Write/Sketch/Illustrate Dream

Pray and ask God....write your interpretation below.
- What is the meaning of the dream?
- What is the purpose of the dream?
- How do I apply the dream to my life?

What other questions do you still have about your dream?

DATE: TITLE:

Describe your dream in 3-5 sentences.

Scene(s): Where is your dream taking place?

Location	Means to You	Positive	Negative

What role do YOU <u>play</u> in dream?   ☐ Observer   ☐ Participant

List the important people and things in your dream.

Person/Thing	Representative	Positive	Negative

©2020 One Neighbor Publishing LLC

Color(s): What colors were in your dream?

Color	Means to You	Positive	Negative

What was on your mind or heart prior to falling asleep? Were you reading or watching anything that found its way in your dream?

List any current issues or decisions pending closure or guidance.

Is this a recurring dream?   Yes ☐   No ☐

If yes, what details stood out?

What emotion(s) were you feeling in the dream?

©2020 One Neighbor Publishing LLC

Write/Sketch/Illustrate Dream

Pray and ask God....write your interpretation below.
- What is the meaning of the dream?
- What is the purpose of the dream?
- How do I apply the dream to my life?

What other questions do you still have about your dream?

DATE: TITLE:

Describe your dream in 3-5 sentences.

Scene(s): Where is your dream taking place?

Location	Means to You	Positive	Negative

What role do YOU play in dream?   ☐ Observer   ☐ Participant

List the important people and things in your dream.

Person/Thing	Representative	Positive	Negative

Color(s): What colors were in your dream?

Color	Means to You	Positive	Negative

What was on your mind or heart prior to falling asleep? Were you reading or watching anything that found its way in your dream?

List any current issues or decisions pending closure or guidance.

Is this a recurring dream?   Yes ☐   No ☐

If yes, what details stood out?

What emotion(s) were you feeling in the dream?

©2020 One Neighbor Publishing LLC

Write/Sketch/Illustrate Dream

Pray and ask God....write your interpretation below.
- What is the meaning of the dream?
- What is the purpose of the dream?
- How do I apply the dream to my life?

What other questions do you still have about your dream?

DATE: TITLE:

Describe your dream in 3-5 sentences.

Scene(s): Where is your dream taking place?

Location	Means to You	Positive	Negative

What role do YOU <u>play</u> in dream? ☐ Observer ☐ Participant

List the important people and things in your dream.

Person/Thing	Representative	Positive	Negative

©2020 One Neighbor Publishing LLC

Color(s): What colors were in your dream?

Color	Means to You	Positive	Negative

What was on your mind or heart prior to falling asleep? Were you reading or watching anything that found its way in your dream?

List any current issues or decisions pending closure or guidance.

Is this a recurring dream?   Yes ☐   No ☐

If yes, what details stood out?

What emotion(s) were you feeling in the dream?

©2020 One Neighbor Publishing LLC

Write/Sketch/Illustrate Dream

©2020 One Neighbor Publishing LLC

Pray and ask God....write your interpretation below.
- What is the meaning of the dream?
- What is the purpose of the dream?
- How do I apply the dream to my life?

What other questions do you still have about your dream?

©2020 One Neighbor Publishing LLC

DATE: TITLE:

Describe your dream in 3-5 sentences.

Scene(s): Where is your dream taking place?

Location	Means to You	Positive	Negative

What role do YOU play in dream? ☐ Observer ☐ Participant

List the important people and things in your dream.

Person/Thing	Representative	Positive	Negative

©2020 One Neighbor Publishing LLC

Color(s): What colors were in your dream?

Color	Means to You	Positive	Negative

What was on your mind or heart prior to falling asleep? Were you reading or watching anything that found its way in your dream?

List any current issues or decisions pending closure or guidance.

Is this a recurring dream? Yes ☐ No ☐

If yes, what details stood out?

What emotion(s) were you feeling in the dream?

©2020 One Neighbor Publishing LLC

Write/Sketch/Illustrate Dream

Pray and ask God....write your interpretation below.
- What is the meaning of the dream?
- What is the purpose of the dream?
- How do I apply the dream to my life?

What other questions do you still have about your dream?

DATE: TITLE:

Describe your dream in 3-5 sentences.

Scene(s): Where is your dream taking place?

Location	Means to You	Positive	Negative

What role do YOU <u>play</u> in dream?   ☐ Observer   ☐ Participant

List the important people and things in your dream.

Person/Thing	Representative	Positive	Negative

©2020 One Neighbor Publishing LLC

Color(s): What colors were in your dream?

Color	Means to You	Positive	Negative

What was on your mind or heart prior to falling asleep? Were you reading or watching anything that found its way in your dream?

List any current issues or decisions pending closure or guidance.

Is this a recurring dream?   Yes ☐   No ☐

If yes, what details stood out?

What emotion(s) were you feeling in the dream?

©2020 One Neighbor Publishing LLC

Write/Sketch/Illustrate Dream

©2020 One Neighbor Publishing LLC

Pray and ask God....write your interpretation below.
- What is the meaning of the dream?
- What is the purpose of the dream?
- How do I apply the dream to my life?

What other questions do you still have about your dream?

DATE: **TITLE:**

Describe your dream in 3-5 sentences.

Scene(s): Where is your dream taking place?

Location	Means to You	Positive	Negative

What role do YOU play in dream? ☐ Observer ☐ Participant

List the important people and things in your dream.

Person/Thing	Representative	Positive	Negative

©2020 One Neighbor Publishing LLC

Color(s): What colors were in your dream?

Color	Means to You	Positive	Negative

What was on your mind or heart prior to falling asleep? Were you reading or watching anything that found its way in your dream?

List any current issues or decisions pending closure or guidance.

Is this a recurring dream?   Yes ☐   No ☐

If yes, what details stood out?

What emotion(s) were you feeling in the dream?

©2020 One Neighbor Publishing LLC

Write/Sketch/Illustrate Dream

Pray and ask God....write your interpretation below.
- What is the meaning of the dream?
- What is the purpose of the dream?
- How do I apply the dream to my life?

What other questions do you still have about your dream?

DATE: TITLE:

Describe your dream in 3-5 sentences.

Scene(s): Where is your dream taking place?

Location	Means to You	Positive	Negative

What role do YOU play in dream?   ☐ Observer   ☐ Participant

List the important people and things in your dream.

Person/Thing	Representative	Positive	Negative

©2020 One Neighbor Publishing LLC

Color(s): What colors were in your dream?

Color	Means to You	Positive	Negative

What was on your mind or heart prior to falling asleep? Were you reading or watching anything that found its way in your dream?

List any current issues or decisions pending closure or guidance.

Is this a recurring dream?   Yes ☐   No ☐

If yes, what details stood out?

What emotion(s) were you feeling in the dream?

©2020 One Neighbor Publishing LLC

Write/Sketch/Illustrate Dream

Pray and ask God....write your interpretation below.
- What is the meaning of the dream?
- What is the purpose of the dream?
- How do I apply the dream to my life?

What other questions do you still have about your dream?

©2020 One Neighbor Publishing LLC

DATE: TITLE:

Describe your dream in 3-5 sentences.

Scene(s): Where is your dream taking place?

Location	Means to You	Positive	Negative

What role do YOU <u>play</u> in dream?   ☐ Observer   ☐ Participant

List the important people and things in your dream.

Person/Thing	Representative	Positive	Negative

©2020 One Neighbor Publishing LLC

Color(s): What colors were in your dream?

Color	Means to You	Positive	Negative

What was on your mind or heart prior to falling asleep? Were you reading or watching anything that found its way in your dream?

List any current issues or decisions pending closure or guidance.

Is this a recurring dream?   Yes ☐   No ☐

If yes, what details stood out?

What emotion(s) were you feeling in the dream?

©2020 One Neighbor Publishing LLC

Write/Sketch/Illustrate Dream

©2020 One Neighbor Publishing LLC

Pray and ask God....write your interpretation below.
- What is the meaning of the dream?
- What is the purpose of the dream?
- How do I apply the dream to my life?

DATE: **TITLE:**

Describe your dream in 3-5 sentences.

Scene(s): Where is your dream taking place?

Location	Means to You	Positive	Negative

What role do YOU <u>play</u> in dream? ☐ Observer ☐ Participant

Color(s): What colors were in your dream?

Color	Means to You	Positive	Negative

What was on your mind or heart prior to falling asleep? Were you reading or watching anything that found its way in your dream?

List any current issues or decisions pending closure or guidance.

Is this a recurring dream?   Yes ☐   No ☐

If yes, what details stood out?

What emotion(s) were you feeling in the dream?

©2020 One Neighbor Publishing LLC

Write/Sketch/Illustrate Dream

Pray and ask God....write your interpretation below.
- What is the meaning of the dream?
- What is the purpose of the dream?
- How do I apply the dream to my life?

What other questions do you still have about your dream?

©2020 One Neighbor Publishing LLC

DATE: **TITLE:**

Describe your dream in 3-5 sentences.

Scene(s): Where is your dream taking place?

Location	Means to You	Positive	Negative

What role do YOU play in dream? ☐ Observer ☐ Participant

List the important people and things in your dream.

Person/Thing	Representative	Positive	Negative

©2020 One Neighbor Publishing LLC

Color(s): What colors were in your dream?

Color	Means to You	Positive	Negative

What was on your mind or heart prior to falling asleep? Were you reading or watching anything that found its way in your dream?

List any current issues or decisions pending closure or guidance.

Is this a recurring dream?   Yes ☐   No ☐

If yes, what details stood out?

What emotion(s) were you feeling in the dream?

©2020 One Neighbor Publishing LLC

Write/Sketch/Illustrate Dream

Pray and ask God....write your interpretation below.
- What is the meaning of the dream?
- What is the purpose of the dream?
- How do I apply the dream to my life?

What other questions do you still have about your dream?

DATE: **TITLE:**

Describe your dream in 3-5 sentences.

Scene(s): Where is your dream taking place?

Location	Means to You	Positive	Negative

What role do YOU play in dream? ☐ Observer ☐ Participant

List the important people and things in your dream.

Person/Thing	Representative	Positive	Negative

©2020 One Neighbor Publishing LLC

Color(s): What colors were in your dream?

Color	Means to You	Positive	Negative

What was on your mind or heart prior to falling asleep? Were you reading or watching anything that found its way in your dream?

List any current issues or decisions pending closure or guidance.

Is this a recurring dream?   Yes ☐   No ☐

If yes, what details stood out?

What emotion(s) were you feeling in the dream?

©2020 One Neighbor Publishing LLC

Write/Sketch/Illustrate Dream

Pray and ask God....write your interpretation below.
- What is the meaning of the dream?
- What is the purpose of the dream?
- How do I apply the dream to my life?

What other questions do you still have about your dream?

Color(s): What colors were in your dream?

Color	Means to You	Positive	Negative

What was on your mind or heart prior to falling asleep? Were you reading or watching anything that found its way in your dream?

List any current issues or decisions pending closure or guidance.

Is this a recurring dream?   Yes ☐   No ☐

If yes, what details stood out?

What emotion(s) were you feeling in the dream?

©2020 One Neighbor Publishing LLC

Write/Sketch/Illustrate Dream

©2020 One Neighbor Publishing LLC

Pray and ask God....write your interpretation below.
- What is the meaning of the dream?
- What is the purpose of the dream?
- How do I apply the dream to my life?

What other questions do you still have about your dream?

©2020 One Neighbor Publishing LLC

DATE: TITLE:

Describe your dream in 3-5 sentences.

Scene(s): Where is your dream taking place?

Location	Means to You	Positive	Negative

What role do YOU <u>play</u> in dream?   ☐ Observer   ☐ Participant

List the important people and things in your dream.

Person/Thing	Representative	Positive	Negative

©2020 One Neighbor Publishing LLC

Color(s): What colors were in your dream?

Color	Means to You	Positive	Negative

What was on your mind or heart prior to falling asleep? Were you reading or watching anything that found its way in your dream?

List any current issues or decisions pending closure or guidance.

Is this a recurring dream? Yes ☐ No ☐

If yes, what details stood out?

What emotion(s) were you feeling in the dream?

©2020 One Neighbor Publishing LLC

Write/Sketch/Illustrate Dream

Pray and ask God....write your interpretation below.
- What is the meaning of the dream?
- What is the purpose of the dream?
- How do I apply the dream to my life?

What other questions do you still have about your dream?

DATE: TITLE:

Describe your dream in 3-5 sentences.

Scene(s): Where is your dream taking place?

Location	Means to You	Positive	Negative

What role do YOU <u>play</u> in dream? ☐ Observer   ☐ Participant

List the important people and things in your dream.

Person/Thing	Representative	Positive	Negative

©2020 One Neighbor Publishing LLC

Color(s): What colors were in your dream?

Color	Means to You	Positive	Negative

What was on your mind or heart prior to falling asleep? Were you reading or watching anything that found its way in your dream?

List any current issues or decisions pending closure or guidance.

Is this a recurring dream?   Yes ☐   No ☐

If yes, what details stood out?

What emotion(s) were you feeling in the dream?

©2020 One Neighbor Publishing LLC

Write/Sketch/Illustrate Dream

©2020 One Neighbor Publishing LLC

Pray and ask God....write your interpretation below.
- What is the meaning of the dream?
- What is the purpose of the dream?
- How do I apply the dream to my life?

What other questions do you still have about your dream?

DATE: TITLE:

Describe your dream in 3-5 sentences.

Scene(s): Where is your dream taking place?

Location	Means to You	Positive	Negative

What role do YOU <u>play</u> in dream?   ☐ Observer   ☐ Participant

List the important people and things in your dream.

Person/Thing	Representative	Positive	Negative

©2020 One Neighbor Publishing LLC

Color(s): What colors were in your dream?

Color	Means to You	Positive	Negative

What was on your mind or heart prior to falling asleep? Were you reading or watching anything that found its way in your dream?

List any current issues or decisions pending closure or guidance.

Is this a recurring dream? Yes ☐ No ☐

If yes, what details stood out?

What emotion(s) were you feeling in the dream?

©2020 One Neighbor Publishing LLC

Write/Sketch/Illustrate Dream

©2020 One Neighbor Publishing LLC

Pray and ask God....write your interpretation below.
- What is the meaning of the dream?
- What is the purpose of the dream?
- How do I apply the dream to my life?

What other questions do you still have about your dream?

DATE: TITLE:

Describe your dream in 3-5 sentences.

Scene(s): Where is your dream taking place?

Location	Means to You	Positive	Negative

What role do YOU <u>play</u> in dream?   ☐ Observer   ☐ Participant

List the important people and things in your dream.

Person/Thing	Representative	Positive	Negative

©2020 One Neighbor Publishing LLC

Color(s): What colors were in your dream?

Color	Means to You	Positive	Negative

What was on your mind or heart prior to falling asleep? Were you reading or watching anything that found its way in your dream?

List any current issues or decisions pending closure or guidance.

Is this a recurring dream?   Yes ☐   No ☐

If yes, what details stood out?

What emotion(s) were you feeling in the dream?

©2020 One Neighbor Publishing LLC

Write/Sketch/Illustrate Dream

©2020 One Neighbor Publishing LLC

Pray and ask God....write your interpretation below.
- What is the meaning of the dream?
- What is the purpose of the dream?
- How do I apply the dream to my life?

What other questions do you still have about your dream?

©2020 One Neighbor Publishing LLC

DATE: TITLE:

Describe your dream in 3-5 sentences.

Scene(s): Where is your dream taking place?

Location	Means to You	Positive	Negative

What role do YOU <u>play</u> in dream?   ☐ Observer   ☐ Participant

List the important people and things in your dream.

Person/Thing	Representative	Positive	Negative

©2020 One Neighbor Publishing LLC

Color(s): What colors were in your dream?

Color	Means to You	Positive	Negative

What was on your mind or heart prior to falling asleep? Were you reading or watching anything that found its way in your dream?

List any current issues or decisions pending closure or guidance.

Is this a recurring dream?   Yes ☐   No ☐

If yes, what details stood out?

What emotion(s) were you feeling in the dream?

©2020 One Neighbor Publishing LLC

Write/Sketch/Illustrate Dream

©2020 One Neighbor Publishing LLC

Pray and ask God....write your interpretation below.
- What is the meaning of the dream?
- What is the purpose of the dream?
- How do I apply the dream to my life?

What other questions do you still have about your dream?

©2020 One Neighbor Publishing LLC

DATE: TITLE:

Describe your dream in 3-5 sentences.

Scene(s): Where is your dream taking place?

Location	Means to You	Positive	Negative

What role do YOU play in dream?   ☐ Observer   ☐ Participant

List the important people and things in your dream.

Person/Thing	Representative	Positive	Negative

©2020 One Neighbor Publishing LLC

Color(s): What colors were in your dream?

Color	Means to You	Positive	Negative

What was on your mind or heart prior to falling asleep? Were you reading or watching anything that found its way in your dream?

List any current issues or decisions pending closure or guidance.

Is this a recurring dream?   Yes ☐   No ☐

If yes, what details stood out?

What emotion(s) were you feeling in the dream?

©2020 One Neighbor Publishing LLC

Write/Sketch/Illustrate Dream

©2020 One Neighbor Publishing LLC

Pray and ask God....write your interpretation below.
- What is the meaning of the dream?
- What is the purpose of the dream?
- How do I apply the dream to my life?

What other questions do you still have about your dream?

©2020 One Neighbor Publishing LLC

DATE: **TITLE:**

Describe your dream in 3-5 sentences.

Scene(s): Where is your dream taking place?

Location	Means to You	Positive	Negative

What role do YOU <u>play</u> in dream?   ☐ Observer   ☐ Participant

List the important people and things in your dream.

Person/Thing	Representative	Positive	Negative

Color(s): What colors were in your dream?

Color	Means to You	Positive	Negative

What was on your mind or heart prior to falling asleep? Were you reading or watching anything that found its way in your dream?

List any current issues or decisions pending closure or guidance.

Is this a recurring dream?   Yes ☐   No ☐

If yes, what details stood out?

What emotion(s) were you feeling in the dream?

©2020 One Neighbor Publishing LLC

Write/Sketch/Illustrate Dream

©2020 One Neighbor Publishing LLC

Pray and ask God....write your interpretation below.
- What is the meaning of the dream?
- What is the purpose of the dream?
- How do I apply the dream to my life?

What other questions do you still have about your dream?

DATE: TITLE:

Describe your dream in 3-5 sentences.

Scene(s): Where is your dream taking place?

Location	Means to You	Positive	Negative

What role do YOU <u>play</u> in dream? ☐ Observer ☐ Participant

List the important people and things in your dream.

Person/Thing	Representative	Positive	Negative

©2020 One Neighbor Publishing LLC

Color(s): What colors were in your dream?

Color	Means to You	Positive	Negative

What was on your mind or heart prior to falling asleep? Were you reading or watching anything that found its way in your dream?

List any current issues or decisions pending closure or guidance.

Is this a recurring dream?   Yes ☐   No ☐

If yes, what details stood out?

What emotion(s) were you feeling in the dream?

©2020 One Neighbor Publishing LLC

Write/Sketch/Illustrate Dream

Pray and ask God....write your interpretation below.
- What is the meaning of the dream?
- What is the purpose of the dream?
- How do I apply the dream to my life?

What other questions do you still have about your dream?

DATE: **TITLE:**

Describe your dream in 3-5 sentences.

Scene(s): Where is your dream taking place?

Location	Means to You	Positive	Negative

What role do YOU <u>play</u> in dream?   ☐ Observer   ☐ Participant

List the important people and things in your dream.

Person/Thing	Representative	Positive	Negative

©2020 One Neighbor Publishing LLC

Color(s): What colors were in your dream?

Color	Means to You	Positive	Negative

What was on your mind or heart prior to falling asleep? Were you reading or watching anything that found its way in your dream?

List any current issues or decisions pending closure or guidance.

Is this a recurring dream?   Yes ☐   No ☐

If yes, what details stood out?

What emotion(s) were you feeling in the dream?

©2020 One Neighbor Publishing LLC

Write/Sketch/Illustrate Dream

Pray and ask God....write your interpretation below.
- What is the meaning of the dream?
- What is the purpose of the dream?
- How do I apply the dream to my life?

What other questions do you still have about your dream?

©2020 One Neighbor Publishing LLC

DATE: TITLE:

Describe your dream in 3-5 sentences.

Scene(s): Where is your dream taking place?

Location	Means to You	Positive	Negative

What role do YOU <u>play</u> in dream? ☐ Observer ☐ Participant

List the important people and things in your dream.

Person/Thing	Representative	Positive	Negative

©2020 One Neighbor Publishing LLC

Color(s): What colors were in your dream?

Color	Means to You	Positive	Negative

What was on your mind or heart prior to falling asleep? Were you reading or watching anything that found its way in your dream?

List any current issues or decisions pending closure or guidance.

Is this a recurring dream?   Yes ☐   No ☐

If yes, what details stood out?

What emotion(s) were you feeling in the dream?

©2020 One Neighbor Publishing LLC

Write/Sketch/Illustrate Dream

©2020 One Neighbor Publishing LLC

Pray and ask God....write your interpretation below.
- What is the meaning of the dream?
- What is the purpose of the dream?
- How do I apply the dream to my life?

What other questions do you still have about your dream?

DATE: TITLE:

Describe your dream in 3-5 sentences.

Scene(s): Where is your dream taking place?

Location	Means to You	Positive	Negative

What role do YOU <u>play</u> in dream? ☐ Observer   ☐ Participant

List the important people and things in your dream.

Person/Thing	Representative	Positive	Negative

©2020 One Neighbor Publishing LLC

Color(s): What colors were in your dream?

Color	Means to You	Positive	Negative

What was on your mind or heart prior to falling asleep? Were you reading or watching anything that found its way in your dream?

List any current issues or decisions pending closure or guidance.

Is this a recurring dream?   Yes ☐   No ☐

If yes, what details stood out?

What emotion(s) were you feeling in the dream?

©2020 One Neighbor Publishing LLC

Write/Sketch/Illustrate Dream

©2020 One Neighbor Publishing LLC

Pray and ask God....write your interpretation below.
- What is the meaning of the dream?
- What is the purpose of the dream?
- How do I apply the dream to my life?

What other questions do you still have about your dream?

DATE: TITLE:

Describe your dream in 3-5 sentences.

Scene(s): Where is your dream taking place?

Location	Means to You	Positive	Negative

What role do YOU <u>play</u> in dream? ☐ Observer ☐ Participant

List the important people and things in your dream.

Person/Thing	Representative	Positive	Negative

©2020 One Neighbor Publishing LLC

Color(s): What colors were in your dream?

Color	Means to You	Positive	Negative

What was on your mind or heart prior to falling asleep? Were you reading or watching anything that found its way in your dream?

List any current issues or decisions pending closure or guidance.

Is this a recurring dream? Yes ☐   No ☐

If yes, what details stood out?

What emotion(s) were you feeling in the dream?

©2020 One Neighbor Publishing LLC

Write/Sketch/Illustrate Dream

©2020 One Neighbor Publishing LLC

Pray and ask God....write your interpretation below.
- What is the meaning of the dream?
- What is the purpose of the dream?
- How do I apply the dream to my life?

What other questions do you still have about your dream?

DATE: **TITLE:**

Describe your dream in 3-5 sentences.

Scene(s): Where is your dream taking place?

Location	Means to You	Positive	Negative

What role do YOU <u>play</u> in dream?   ☐ Observer   ☐ Participant

List the important people and things in your dream.

Person/Thing	Representative	Positive	Negative

©2020 One Neighbor Publishing LLC

Color(s): What colors were in your dream?

Color	Means to You	Positive	Negative

What was on your mind or heart prior to falling asleep? Were you reading or watching anything that found its way in your dream?

List any current issues or decisions pending closure or guidance.

Is this a recurring dream?   Yes ☐   No ☐

If yes, what details stood out?

What emotion(s) were you feeling in the dream?

©2020 One Neighbor Publishing LLC

Write/Sketch/Illustrate Dream

©2020 One Neighbor Publishing LLC

Pray and ask God....write your interpretation below.
- What is the meaning of the dream?
- What is the purpose of the dream?
- How do I apply the dream to my life?

What other questions do you still have about your dream?

DATE: TITLE:

Describe your dream in 3-5 sentences.

Scene(s): Where is your dream taking place?

Location	Means to You	Positive	Negative

What role do YOU <u>play</u> in dream? ☐ Observer   ☐ Participant

List the important people and things in your dream.

Person/Thing	Representative	Positive	Negative

©2020 One Neighbor Publishing LLC

Color(s): What colors were in your dream?

Color	Means to You	Positive	Negative

What was on your mind or heart prior to falling asleep? Were you reading or watching anything that found its way in your dream?

List any current issues or decisions pending closure or guidance.

Is this a recurring dream?   Yes ☐   No ☐

If yes, what details stood out?

What emotion(s) were you feeling in the dream?

©2020 One Neighbor Publishing LLC

Write/Sketch/Illustrate Dream

Pray and ask God....write your interpretation below.
- What is the meaning of the dream?
- What is the purpose of the dream?
- How do I apply the dream to my life?

What other questions do you still have about your dream?

DATE: TITLE:

Describe your dream in 3-5 sentences.

Scene(s): Where is your dream taking place?

Location	Means to You	Positive	Negative

What role do YOU play in dream?   ☐ Observer   ☐ Participant

List the important people and things in your dream.

Person/Thing	Representative	Positive	Negative

©2020 One Neighbor Publishing LLC

Color(s): What colors were in your dream?

Color	Means to You	Positive	Negative

What was on your mind or heart prior to falling asleep? Were you reading or watching anything that found its way in your dream?

List any current issues or decisions pending closure or guidance.

Is this a recurring dream?   Yes ☐   No ☐

If yes, what details stood out?

What emotion(s) were you feeling in the dream?

©2020 One Neighbor Publishing LLC

Write/Sketch/Illustrate Dream

Pray and ask God....write your interpretation below.
- What is the meaning of the dream?
- What is the purpose of the dream?
- How do I apply the dream to my life?

What other questions do you still have about your dream?

DATE: **TITLE:**

Describe your dream in 3-5 sentences.

Scene(s): Where is your dream taking place?

Location	Means to You	Positive	Negative

What role do YOU play in dream? ☐ Observer ☐ Participant

List the important people and things in your dream.

Person/Thing	Representative	Positive	Negative

Color(s): What colors were in your dream?

Color	Means to You	Positive	Negative

What was on your mind or heart prior to falling asleep? Were you reading or watching anything that found its way in your dream?

List any current issues or decisions pending closure or guidance.

Is this a recurring dream? Yes ☐ No ☐

If yes, what details stood out?

What emotion(s) were you feeling in the dream?

©2020 One Neighbor Publishing LLC

Write/Sketch/Illustrate Dream

©2020 One Neighbor Publishing LLC

Pray and ask God....write your interpretation below.
- What is the meaning of the dream?
- What is the purpose of the dream?
- How do I apply the dream to my life?

What other questions do you still have about your dream?

©2020 One Neighbor Publishing LLC

www.ingramcontent.com/pod-product-compliance
Lightning Source LLC
Chambersburg PA
CBHW081154290426
44108CB00018B/2551